DWAYNE "THE ROCK" JOHNSON

DWAYNE "THE ROCK" JOHNSON

From Wrestler to Hollywood Hero

Matt Doeden

LERNER PUBLICATIONS ◆ MINNEAPOLIS

Lerner Publications Company
An imprint of Lerner Publishing Group, Inc.
241 First Avenue North
Minneapolis, MN 55401 USA

For reading levels and more information, look up this title at www.lernerbooks.com.

Main body text set in Rotis Serif Std 55 Regular. Typeface provided by Adobe Systems.

Image credits: AP Photo/Xavier Collin, Cover; AP Photo/Chris O'Meara, p. 2; AP Photo/Sthanlee B. Mirador, p. 6; Globe Photos/Alamy Stock Photo, p. 8; Unknown photographer/Alamy Stock Photo, p. 10; ARCHIVIO GBB/Alamy Stock Photo, p. 12; George Napolitano/Alamy Stock Photo, p. 13; Jed Jacobsohn/Getty Images, p. 14; Damian Strohmeyer/Sports Illustrated/Getty Images, p. 16; Octavio Jones/Alamy Stock Photo, p. 19; George Pimentel/WireImage/Getty Images, p. 22; Frank Micelotta/Getty Images, p. 23; David Bro/Alamy Stock Photo, p. 24; Keith Hamshere/Universal Studios/Getty Images, p. 26; John Barrett/Alamy Stock Photo, p. 27; Jeff Snyder/FilmMagic/Getty Images, p. 28; WENN/Alamy Stock Photo, pp. 29,30; Eugene Gologursky/WireImage/Getty Images, p. 32; Amy Graves/Getty Images, p. 33; Kevin Winter/Getty Images, p. 34; Yui Mok/Alamy Stock Photo, p. 35; PictureLux/Alamy Stock Photo, p. 36; Karwai Tang/WireImage/Getty Images, p. 37; Jesse Grant/Getty Images for Disney, p. 39; Barry King/Alamy Stock Photo, p. 40; Greg Doherty/Getty Images, p. 41.

Editor: Karen Latchana Kenney **Designer:** Lauren Cooper

Library of Congress Cataloging-in-Publication Data

Names: Doeden, Matt, author.
Title: Dwayne "The Rock" Johnson : from wrestler to Hollywood hero / Matt Doeden.
Description: Minneapolis : Lerner Publications, 2023. | Series: Gateway biographies | Includes bibliographical references and index. | Audience: Ages 9–14 | Audience: Grades 4–6 | Summary: "He isn't just a phenomenal professional wrestler. Dwayne "The Rock" Johnson is also a businessperson and one of the most successful American actors ever. Follow his career from college football player to international superstar"– Provided by publisher.
Identifiers: LCCN 2022021703 (print) | LCCN 2022021704 (ebook) | ISBN 9781728476575 (library binding) | ISBN 9781728486338 (paperback) | ISBN 9781728482743 (ebook)
Subjects: LCSH: Johnson, Dwayne, 1972-–Juvenile literature. | Wrestlers–United States–Biography–Juvenile literature. | Actors–United States–Biography–Juvenile literature. | LCGFT: Biographies.
Classification: LCC GV1196.J64 D64 2023 (print) | LCC GV1196.J64 (ebook) | DDC 796.812092 [B]–dc23/eng/20220512

LC record available at https://lccn.loc.gov/2022021703
LC ebook record available at https://lccn.loc.gov/2022021704

Manufactured in the United States of America
3-1009742-50678-5/31/2023

TABLE OF CONTENTS

Dwayne Johnson arrives at Disney's *Jungle Cruise* world premiere held at Disneyland in Anaheim, California, on July 24, 2021.

The crowd roared as The Rock marched toward the ring for the main event of WrestleMania X-Seven (17). On April 1, 2001, the biggest event of the year for the World Wrestling Entertainment (WWE) was underway. The clash was between two of wrestling's biggest stars. "Stone Cold" Steve Austin had been the face of the WWE for years. But a new challenger had emerged. Dwayne Johnson—better known as The Rock—was the hottest WWE up-and-comer.

The epic clash for the WWE Championship was held before a record crowd of more than sixty thousand fans. The two stars of the WWE were battling in a no-disqualification match—so nothing was off-limits, and only a pin would end the match.

Austin pins The Rock during their WrestleMania match.

Of course, as Austin and The Rock faced off, both knew what the result would be. The WWE and WrestleMania have scripted events. Each wrestler plays a character, carefully crafted to maximize the drama and the crowd's emotional reaction. Yet none of that mattered to the tens of thousands of screaming fans in the arena. As the two powerful men met in the center of the ring, the battle was on.

The action was high-flying and brutal. The wrestlers, drenched in sweat, fought inside and outside the ring.

Austin would take the advantage, only to have The Rock suddenly reverse the stakes. Back and forth they fought, keeping the crowd on its feet.

Late in the match, The Rock stung Austin with one of his signature moves—the People's Elbow—usually a big finisher for the young star. He quickly covered up Austin for the pin.

Of course, in pro wrestling, it's never that simple. WWE chairman and CEO Vince McMahon wanted Austin to win. So, he grabbed The Rock, pulling him off Austin just long enough for the wrestler to recover. The match went on.

Over the next several minutes, The Rock had to battle both Austin and McMahon. Normally, it would have been a violation of the rules. But this was a no-disqualification match. No one could do anything to stop the cheating.

Austin hit The Rock with his own signature move, the Stone Cold Stunner. He went for the pin, but The Rock kicked out. Once again, McMahon stepped in. He gave Austin a steel chair. Austin pummeled The Rock with the chair, leaving him bloody and beaten. Austin finally completed the pin to end the match and claim the WWE Championship.

The match was a loss for The Rock. But it was also one of his greatest moments. To this day, many wrestling fans list WrestleMania X-Seven as the greatest of all time and the clash between Austin and The Rock as its peak. A new period in the WWE was underway. It was the era of The Rock.

Early Life

Dwayne Douglas Johnson was born on May 2, 1972, in Haywood, California. Wrestling was in his blood. His dad, Rocky Johnson, had been a pro wrestler in the WWE. His mom, Ata Johnson, was the daughter of Peter Maivia, a Samoan wrestler.

Dwayne was the couple's only child. From the time he was little, he was surrounded by wrestling. He'd watch his dad perform in WWE matches. He would play with Rocky's championship belts and practice his own moves.

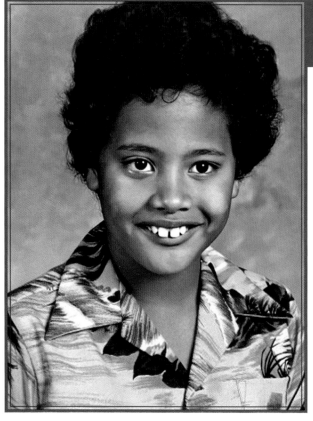

Young Dwayne came from a well-known wrestling family.

"I was fascinated by the business," Johnson later wrote. "I loved everything about it: the violence, the theatricality, the athleticism, the volume . . . everything."

Life wasn't easy, though. As the elder Johnson moved from job to job, the family was frequently moving. By the time Dwayne was thirteen, he'd already lived in thirteen different states. As he became a teenager, Dwayne had some behavior problems. He argued with his parents. He got in trouble at school, often for fighting. He was arrested for stealing jewelry. It was a difficult time in his life.

One thing that helped keep Dwayne anchored was sports. He loved to spend time in the weight room, building muscle. He was a good athlete, excelling in track and field. Football was his best sport. His size, strength, and speed made him a star defensive tackle on the field.

By the time he was sixteen, Dwayne stood 6 feet 4 inches (1.9 m) tall and weighed 225 pounds (102 kg). Most of that weight was solid muscle. Dwayne had played football at several high schools already. But when the family moved to Bethlehem, Pennsylvania, and he started attending Freedom High School, football became something more. Dwayne started to see the sport as a way to achieve a better life.

"I fell in love with the game," he said. "It gave my life a purpose. . . . Suddenly I had a chance to become the first person in my family to go to college. I became obsessed with making it."

In high school, Dwayne showed his athletic skills on the football field.

Dwayne was a natural. His powerful frame allowed him to tear through opponents' offensive lines. He was the defensive star of his high school team.

Dwayne's success on the football field gained him a lot of attention. Many of the top colleges in the nation recruited him to join their football teams. He got scholarship offers from Penn State, the University of California, Los Angeles (UCLA), Florida State, and others.

The school he really wanted to attend was the University of Miami. But Dennis Erickson, the coach of the Miami Hurricanes, wasn't recruiting Dwayne. So, Dwayne called the school's recruiter and explained how he could help the team. Erickson took notice. The coach offered Dwayne a full scholarship. Dwayne had done it. Instead of waiting for an offer to come to him, he'd gone out and paved his own way. This personality trait would mark much of his career and life to follow.

ROCKY JOHNSON

Rocky Johnson—born Wayde Douglas Bowles—gained fame in wrestling, but he started his career in the boxing ring. Johnson

sparred with boxing legends George Foreman and Muhammad Ali before turning to wrestling. He took his name from two of his favorite boxers, Rocky Marciano and Jack Johnson.

Rocky Johnson starred in the National Wrestling Alliance for almost two decades before switching to the WWE in 1982. He teamed with Tony Atlas to win the Tag Team Championship in 1983—a monumental win. Together, they became the first Black athletes to hold a WWE belt. Johnson officially retired from pro wrestling in 1991.

Welcome to Miami

In the fall of 1990, Johnson enrolled at the University of Miami. The Hurricanes were one of the best college teams in the country. They'd won the national championship a year before. The Hurricanes roster was stacked with future National Football League (NFL) talent.

Johnson knew it would be tough to earn playing time as a freshman. But he impressed his coaches. "He was strong, he could use his hands, he was tough as nails, and he worked his [butt] off," said then defensive line coach Ed Orgeron. "[Johnson] was a [heck of a] football player. I thought he had a chance to be an All-American."

Johnson was on track to be a starter for the team. But then disaster struck. He badly injured his shoulder during practice. While

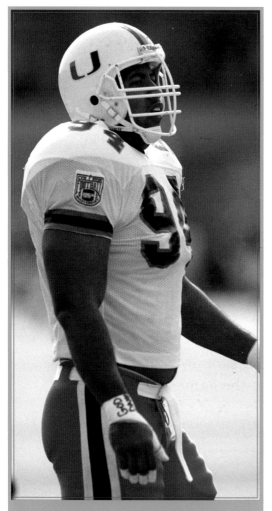

Johnson was #94 on the Miami Hurricanes football team.

he recovered, another up-and-coming star, Warren Sapp, took his place. Sapp stepped into the starting role and dominated. Johnson never got another chance to start at Miami. When his shoulder healed, he returned as Sapp's backup. Sapp went on to have a Hall-of-Fame NFL career.

Even as a backup, Johnson enjoyed success with Miami. The 1991 season was one to remember. The Hurricanes went 12–0 and won the national championship. Johnson went on to play four seasons with Miami. During that time, he played in thirty-nine games, but started in just one game. He ended his college career with seventy-seven tackles and four sacks.

The most memorable play of his career came in a 1993 game against Florida State. Johnson lined up on the interior of the defensive line. His job was to rush Florida State quarterback Charlie Ward. Ward was the best player in college football that year and went on to win the Heisman Trophy. But when Ward took the snap, Johnson was off. He slipped past his blocker to the outside. Then he charged from Ward's blind side. The quarterback couldn't get out of the way. Johnson drove him to the turf for a sack. It was a big play in the game, but it wasn't enough for Miami. Florida State went on to win, 28–10.

The sack was one of a few flashes of greatness Johnson showed at Miami. But injuries and a lack of playing time held him back. Some of his teammates believed that if he'd gone to another school, where he wasn't stuck behind Sapp on the depth chart, he could have developed into an NFL-caliber player.

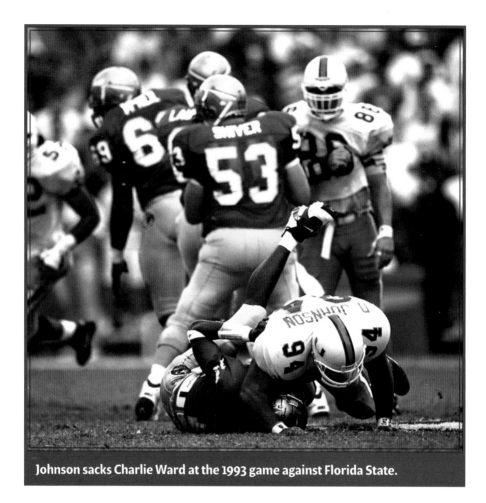
Johnson sacks Charlie Ward at the 1993 game against Florida State.

But that didn't happen. It's something that Johnson never forgot. "I'd always had a very specific vision of my future," he said later. "I was going to be [football star] Michael Strahan: I would win a Super Bowl. . . . I think about it all the time: What if I had been a little better at football? . . . But I didn't get to walk away [from football] on my terms, and that lit a fire that still burns. I wanted that life I had envisioned, but I had to find another way."

THE MiAMi HURRiCANES

The University of Miami has one of the most successful college football programs in the United States. Johnson played for the Hurricanes during the team's peak. The school won all five of its national championships in a span from 1983 to 2001. The Hurricanes play their home games in Hard Rock Stadium in Miami Gardens, Florida. On game days, the stadium can be packed with more than sixty-five thousand fans, most wearing the team's orange, green, and white colors.

From the Field to the Mat

Johnson graduated from the University of Miami in 1995. He earned a degree in criminology and physiology. For a time, Johnson thought he might use his degree to pursue a career with the Central Intelligence Agency (CIA). But he never really explored that path. He still had his sights set on professional football.

The 1995 NFL Draft came and went. Nobody selected Johnson. It wasn't a surprise. He hadn't played enough in college to catch the attention of NFL scouts. Johnson didn't give up though. He signed with the Calgary

Stampeders of the Canadian Football League (CFL) as a linebacker. The CFL was a step below the NFL in talent and level of competition. But it had served as a springboard for a handful of players who went on to good NFL careers. Johnson hoped he could follow that same route. He earned a spot on Calgary's practice squad. But his hopes of impressing in the CFL quickly dimmed. He didn't get any playing time and was cut from the team a few months later.

It was becoming clear to Johnson that his dream to play in the NFL was not going to be a reality. He was broke. He was out of work. It was time to move on. He decided to go back to his roots. Johnson asked his dad to teach him the tricks of the wrestling trade. The pair worked together, honing Johnson's skills and working on his moves in the ring. Soon, Johnson was performing in shows at fairs and other small venues. He didn't earn much money—about thirty-five dollars a night. But it was a chance to keep working on his moves and develop the personality that he would use with his characters inside and outside of the wrestling ring.

For most people, pro wrestling is tough to break into. But Johnson's family gave him the connections he needed to earn a tryout with the WWE, the biggest wrestling company in the world. And Johnson had a lot of the traits that make a great wrestler. He was big, powerful, and athletic. He was comfortable in front of a microphone and had a strong personality. And because he'd grown up around wrestling, he understood how the business worked.

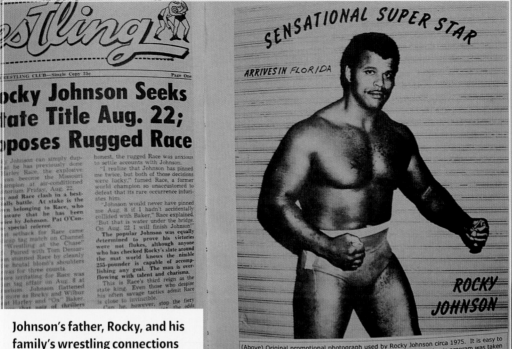

Johnson's father, Rocky, and his family's wrestling connections helped him break into the WWE.

(Above) Original promotional photograph used by Rocky Johnson circa 1975. It is easy to detect the handwritten "Florida." Note the photo used in the St. Louis program was taken in the same location as this promotional photograph.

In 1996 Johnson got his break. He signed with the WWE. At first, he wrestled in a developmental league, the United States Wrestling Alliance—a training ground for up-and-coming WWE talent. Johnson took on the stage name Flex Kavana. "I don't know who came up with that name or where it came from," said wrestling legend Jerry Lawler. "But anyway, he was Flex Kavana."

Kavana, an ultracool baby face (a "good guy" in wrestling), came with a stylish haircut and a pair of sunglasses. Lawler took an active role in helping Johnson, grooming him for a bigger stage.

WRESTLING PERSONAS

In professional wrestling, most wrestlers play characters, or personas, rather than themselves. A persona often focuses on a few characteristics that define the wrestler. For example, Flex Kavana was all about style, with a slick hairstyle, sunglasses, and cool attitude. Wrestling has been filled with memorable personas through the years. The Undertaker was a dark, mysterious giant. Ric Flair bragged about his skill and money. Hulk Hogan brought a growl and intensity to his character inside the ring and on the microphone. Personas help give wrestlers identities that are easy for fans to love—or hate.

"There aren't many people you can say were really naturals but The Rock was," Lawler said. "It was in his heritage. . . . [Johnson] grew up around that and I guess that's where it came from. We knew from the get-go that the kid was gonna be something special."

WWE officials liked what they saw. They called Johnson up. He made his WWE television debut on November 17, 1996, in an event called Survivor Series in New York City's Madison Square Garden. But Flex Kavana was gone. WWE officials convinced Johnson to embrace his family's wrestling background instead.

He wrestled under the name Rocky Maivia. The new stage name combined his father's first name and his maternal grandfather's last name.

In the event, Maivia took part in an eight-man match. The last wrestler standing would be the winner. One after the next, other wrestlers went down. At the end, only Maivia and Goldust remained. The two battled it out, and Maivia got the pin to earn a victory in his first match.

The Rock Is Born

Maivia had begun his career as a baby face. He had a clean-cut image and fit the good-guy mold. But in the WWE, his character took a different turn. He became a heel, or a "bad guy." Fans loved to boo him whenever he stepped into the ring. Maivia played up the bad-guy role. He enjoyed getting the crowd riled up.

In 1997 Johnson changed his wrestling name. He was no longer Rocky Maivia. Instead, he called himself simply The Rock. The Rock was a classic heel. He fought dirty. He insulted fellow wrestlers and even the audience. It was all an act, of course. The Rock was a character, and Johnson played him perfectly. His skill on the microphone and his sense of humor made him a fan favorite, even if he played a villain. He showed why a successful wrestler can't just be a great athlete. Acting skills are every bit as important, and Johnson's acting was making him one of the WWE's biggest stars.

At Survivor Series 1998, The Rock won his first WWE Championship. It's the most important belt in the WWE, and the league usually reserves it for the biggest names. After just two years in the WWE, The Rock was already at the top and clearly there to stay. Signature moves like the Rock Bottom and the People's Elbow got fans on their feet. Meanwhile, the catchphrase, "If you smell what The Rock is cooking . . ." gained pop culture status even beyond wrestling fans. Over the decades, a handful of pro wrestlers had become crossover stars, earning fame beyond their wrestling personas. The Rock was following in the steps of Hulk Hogan, "Stone Cold" Steve Austin, and others who made that leap.

During his "heel" phase, The Rock wrestled Hulk Hogan.

The Rock gained more fame after his first WWE Championship win.

Wrestling is only part of the draw of the WWE. Pro wrestling really thrives on a heavy dose of drama. Feuds, scandals, and surprise twists drive the story line as much as the action in the ring. Like most wrestlers, The Rock took turns as a heel and a baby face, with the changes scripted to be as shocking as possible.

Johnson's professional life was changing rapidly. So was his personal life. In 1997 he married businessperson Dany Garcia. Four years later, the couple welcomed their first child, Simone. Johnson devoted himself to his daughter. "Being a father is the greatest job I have ever had and the greatest job I will ever have," he told *People* magazine. "I always wanted to be a great dad. I always wanted to give Simone things that I felt I never got."

THE FAMILY LEGACY

In 2020 Simone announced that she planned to carry on the family's legacy. Johnson's oldest daughter signed a contract with the WWE. That made her the first fourth-generation wrestler in WWE history. "To know that my family has such a personal connection to wrestling is really special to me . . . ," she said. "I feel grateful to have the opportunity, not only to wrestle, but to carry on that legacy."

Crossing Over

Johnson's acting ability set him apart from many of the other wrestlers in the WWE. Soon the entertainment industry noticed. Johnson started getting roles outside of wrestling. In 1999 he played the role of his dad on the popular TV series *That 70s Show.* A year later, he played the part of a wrestling alien on *Star Trek: Voyager* and hosted the iconic comedy show *Saturday Night Live.*

It was just the beginning of a new career. In 2001 Johnson made his motion-picture debut in *The Mummy Returns.* The film was a sequel to the popular 1999 film *The Mummy.* Johnson played the role of the Scorpion King, a villain who tries to conquer the world. The film was a box-office hit. It made $435 million globally, although it was poorly received by most movie critics. Johnson won a Teen Choice Award for best movie villain. But The Stinkers Bad Movie Awards also named him Worst Supporting Actor.

The mixed reviews didn't slow down the *Mummy* franchise. In 2002 Universal Pictures released a new film, *The Scorpion King,* based around Johnson's character. Film critic Roger Ebert gave Johnson a positive review. "[*The Scorpion King*] has high energy," Ebert wrote. "The action never stops, the dialogue knows it's funny, and The Rock has the authority to play the role and the fortitude to keep a straight face. I expect him to become a durable action star."

Johnson followed up his success in the *Mummy* franchise with roles in *The Rundown* (2003) and *Walking*

Johnson's first motion picture role was in *The Mummy Returns*.

Tall (2004). Neither film was a box-office smash. But they gave Johnson a chance to explore his acting potential and show himself as one of Hollywood's new action stars.

While Johnson's acting career was taking off, he continued to be one of the biggest names in the WWE. He kept piling up belts, yet his place as one of the most popular wrestlers in the WWE was fading. Some fans felt that he was more interested in his acting career than he was in wrestling. By 2002 his fan support was all but gone. The audience booed him after a big victory over Hulk Hogan at WrestleMania. Those boos only grew louder over the next year.

In 2004 The Rock's contract with the WWE ended. It was time for him to focus on the next stage of his career. He was ready to turn his full attention to acting.

In 2002 The Rock was losing popularity in the WWE.

The Big Screen

Over the next decade, Johnson built on his role as one of Hollywood's biggest action stars. In 2005 he appeared as a villain, Sergeant Asher Mahonin, in *Doom*. The movie, based on a popular video game series, was a dud, and critics hated it.

In 2006 Johnson starred in a movie that brought him back to his younger days as a football star. In *Gridiron Gang,* he played the role of Sean Porter, a worker at a juvenile detention center. Porter searched for a way to help kids stay out of trouble after their release. His solution was to start a football team. The film tracks the real-life story of the team, the Kilpatrick Mustangs.

Gridiron Gang screened at Andrews Air Force Base, where Johnson met with troops.

The dramatic role was something new for Johnson, who had been largely limited to action films. It was the kind of step he'd wanted to take. "When I first started acting, my goal was to become a really good versatile actor," he explained. "But five years ago, I certainly was not getting the kind of material that allowed me to do that. I knew I had to just be really choosy about my roles with the material that I was given."

Gridiron Gang didn't do well at the box office, but Johnson earned some praise for his performance. "Dwayne Johnson pushes his emotionally charged performance so hard that you think he might pop a blood vessel," wrote film critic Cole Smithey. Johnson's football theme continued in 2007 when he starred as a player in *The Game Plan*.

Johnson also branched out into comedy. His sense of humor and timing earned him parts in comedies such as *Reno 911! Miami* (2007) and *Get Smart* (2008). Around this time, Johnson made a big change. Until the late 2000s, he was credited as The Rock in his movie roles. Using his famous wrestling persona was a good way to get name recognition at the box office. But he wanted to leave that persona behind. He didn't want to be a wrestler who also acted. He wanted his acting to stand on its own. So, he began acting under his real name. The Rock became the wrestler, while Dwayne Johnson was the actor.

In *Get Smart*, Johnson acted alongside Steve Carell and Anne Hathaway.

Meanwhile, big changes were happening in Johnson's personal life. In 2007 he and Garcia split up, although they remained friends and continued to work together to raise Simone. Johnson found a new love, Lauren Hashian. He met her on the set of *The Game Plan*. The couple later married and had two daughters, Jasmine and Tiana.

A Furious Pace

In 2011 Johnson appeared in what many consider his most iconic film role. He played US agent Luke Hobbs in the fifth installment of the popular *Fast & Furious* movie franchise. The movie, *Fast Five*, was wall-to-wall action centered on fast cars and wild driving stunts.

Johnson signs autographs at the German premier of *Fast Five*.

The film was a success, earning more than $600 million worldwide. It also fared well with critics, who praised its cast, special effects, and relentless action. Nick de Semlyen of *Empire* magazine gave Johnson much of the credit for the film's success. "How to re-ignite an ageing franchise?" he wrote. "Drop The Rock on it. The best thing, by far, in *Fast Five* . . .. Dwayne Johnson hulks through the movie leaving [macho] trails in his wake."

Johnson's acting career was at an all-time high with the release of *Fast Five*. He had left his wrestling persona behind and built a new career. So, it came as a surprise to many when he returned to the WWE in February 2011.

Johnson appeared on the popular program *WWE Raw* to announce that he would host WrestleMania XXVII. Meanwhile, he started a feud with John Cena, who had become the face of the WWE after The Rock left. The WWE spent much of the next year building up the feud between the two megastars. The story line peaked in an action-filled championship match at WrestleMania 29, where Cena defeated The Rock after a hard-hitting, drama-filled match.

The feud between The Rock and Cena may have continued. But Johnson suffered a serious injury during the match, tearing several muscles in his abdomen. The forty-year-old needed surgery to repair the damage, and his return to wrestling had to be put on hold. He would make occasional returns to the WWE over the next six years, but his time as a regular wrestler was over.

At WrestleMania 29, The Rock faced John Cena (*far right*) in the ring.

With the success of *Fast Five*, the *Fast & Furious* movie franchise was alive and well. In 2013 Johnson returned as Luke Hobbs for *Fast & Furious 6*. It followed the same blueprint as the previous films in the series and enjoyed similar success, pulling in $789 million. The character of Hobbs lived on, with Johnson's character returning for multiple films over much of the next decade.

HONORING HIS CULTURE

Body art is important to Johnson. One of his tattoos, on his chest and right arm, honors his Samoan heritage. It includes

coconut leaves (a symbol for a Samoan chief-warrior) and swirls that represent the past, present, and future. Two eyes, called "O mata e lua," stand for ancestors watching over Johnson.

New Projects

In 2013 Johnson produced and hosted a reality TV show called *The Hero*. The show featured contestants who competed in a range of physical and mental challenges for prize money. The eight-episode season aired on the TNT network. It struggled to attract viewers and was canceled after one season.

The Hero wasn't Johnson's only attempt in television. Later, he served as executive producer of the HBO series *Ballers*, which premiered in 2015. He also starred in it, playing Spencer Strasmore, a former NFL player who manages the finances of current players. Over five seasons, the show tracks Strasmore's rise in the NFL, all the way to becoming a team owner.

The show was a huge hit. Critics praised it and gave Johnson much of the credit for its success. "The real find here is Johnson, whose years in film give him a

Johnson's acting in *Ballers* won him a People's Choice Award in 2017.

surprisingly warm and relatable charm on TV," wrote National Public Radio's Eric Deggans. "The world of blockbuster movies might write bigger paychecks, but The Rock may have missed his calling as a television star with the skill to keep a character compelling week after week."

Johnson's TV work did not slow down his production on the big screen. In 2014 he played the title role in the action-adventure film *Hercules*. Two years later, he took a comedic role in *Central Intelligence*, with costar Kevin Hart.

SELFIE BLITZ

At the 2015 London, England, premiere of the film *San Andreas*, Johnson was on a mission. He wanted to be in *Guinness World Records* for the most selfies taken in three minutes. Fans lined up for the rapid-fire selfie session. By the time it was over, Johnson had taken selfies with 105 different fans—a new record. Johnson's mark didn't stand long. Actor Donnie Wahlberg broke it just a year later.

DWAYNE JOHNSON
AS MAUI

AULI'I CRAVALHO
AS MOANA

FROM THE CREATORS OF
ZOOTOPIA & FROZEN

DISNEP

M☺ANA

NOVEMBER 23
IN 3D AND REAL D 3D

In *Moana*, Johnson was the voice of Maui (*right*).

In 2016 Johnson explored a new type of acting. He was cast as the voice of Maui in the animated Disney film *Moana*. The film follows the journey of a young girl, Moana, as she struggles to bring life back to a dying island. Johnson's character, Maui, is a shape-shifting god who helps Moana along the way.

The film was a critical success. It also brought out a side of Johnson that was completely new to most of his fans. Like many Disney films, *Moana* was filled with catchy musical numbers. Maui, as one of the main characters, had his own song, "You're Welcome." The song went platinum four times, or sold more than four million copies worldwide.

Johnson had a hard time believing that his singing voice had gained him so much attention. And he wasn't the only one. His daughter, Tiana, was two years old when she saw the film. She'd beg her dad to sing the song nonstop. According to Johnson, Tiana didn't really believe that her dad was the voice of Maui in the beloved movie.

Johnson was quickly earning a reputation as one of the hardest-working actors in Hollywood. From 2017 to 2018, he starred in five movies. The most successful was *Jumanji: Welcome to the Jungle.* He played the role of archaeologist Dr. Xander "Smolder" Bravestone. The film

At the United Kingdom premier, actors and the director of *Jumanji: Welcome to the Jungle* promoted the movie.

was a massive success in the box office. It brought in $962 million worldwide and got generally positive reviews from critics. The role earned Johnson a Nickelodeon Kids' Choice Award for Favorite Movie Actor and a Teen Choice Award for Choice Movie Actor: Comedy. The movie inspired a sequel, 2019's *Jumanji: The Next Level*. It also did well at the box office.

The Rock Keeps Rolling

Over the years, Johnson continued to make occasional appearances in the WWE. In August 2019, he announced his retirement from the sport.

On the big screen, Johnson kept pumping out films. Although the COVID-19 pandemic slowed down the movie industry in 2020 and 2021, Johnson barely stopped working. In 2021 he starred in *Jungle Cruise*, a film based on the popular Disney World ride of the same name. That year he also appeared in the Netflix film *Red Notice*, playing an FBI agent who teams up with an art thief to catch a criminal.

In 2021 Johnson also embarked on something brand new. He signed with NBC to produce *Young Rock*, a show about his upbringing. Johnson plays himself in the series, while other actors play him at different ages during his childhood.

According to Johnson, creating the show was difficult. His father died while the show was in its early stages of

Johnson promoted the movie *Jungle Cruise* for Walt Disney Studios in 2019.

production. Johnson wanted to tell his story as accurately as possible—even when the truth wasn't pretty. It was an emotional time, but Johnson says he's happy with the result.

"My dad and I, we had a complicated relationship," Johnson told the *New York Times*. "It was very tough love. Let's show the flaws, but when people aren't here anymore, let's show the good stuff, too."

Young Rock is Johnson's new hit television series.

Young Rock appealed to audiences and critics alike. In April 2021, NBC renewed the show for a second and third season.

Like a wrestling match, Johnson's career is full of twists and turns. He's been a football star, a wrestling icon, an action-film star, and the center of a heartfelt biographical television show. He's part athlete, part stunt performer, and part comedian. What's next for one of

With his many talents, Johnson's future is filled with possibilities.

Hollywood's biggest leading men? It's hard to guess. One thing seems certain. Whether as The Rock, Dwayne Johnson, or something new entirely, he's sure to surprise us.

IMPORTANT DATES

1972 Johnson is born on May 2 in Haywood, California.

1990 Johnson is one of the nation's top-rated high school defensive tackles.

1991 Johnson joins the University of Miami football team. He serves as a backup on the team that wins the NCAA national championship.

1993 Johnson sacks Heisman Trophy–winning quarterback Charlie Ward in a loss to Florida State.

1995 Johnson graduates from the University of Miami. He signs with the Calgary Stampeders of the CFL but is cut several months later.

1996 Johnson signs a contract with the WWE. He makes his television debut on November 17.

1997 Johnson adopts a new wrestling name, The Rock.

1998 The Rock wins his first WWE Championship.

2001 Johnson makes his motion-picture debut in *The Mummy Returns*.

2004 Johnson leaves the WWE to focus on his acting career.

2011 Johnson appears in *Fast Five* as agent Luke Hobbs. He returns to the role several times over the next decade.

Johnson returns to the WWE.

2013 Johnson tears several muscles at WrestleMania, ending his time as a WWE regular.

2015 The HBO series *Ballers* debuts. Johnson plays the role of an ex-player who rises to power in the league.

2016 Johnson is the voice of Maui in *Moana* and records the song "You're Welcome" for the film.

2021 The NBC show *Young Rock* debuts to critical acclaim. The show follows Johnson's upbringing.

SOURCE NOTES

11   Dwayne Johnson and Joseph Layden, *The Rock Says . . .* (New York: HarperCollins, 2000), 13.

11   SI staff, "Dwayne Johnson, Almighty Baller," *Sports Illustrated*, December 5, 2016, https://vault.si.com/vault/2016/12/05/dwayne-johnson-almighty-baller.

14   SI staff.

16   Alan Shipnuck, "How Football Helped Transform Dwayne Johnson into Hollywood's Biggest Star," SI.com, November 30, 2016, https://www.si.com/media/2016/11/30/dwayne-johnson-the-rock-nfl-wrestling-hollywood-star.

19   Anthony Benigno, "The Last Stand of Flex Kavana: How Jerry Lawler Got The Rock out of Memphis on 2 Days' Notice," https://WWE.com, November 16, 2016, https://www.wwe.com/superstars/the-rock/article/the-rock-jerry-lawler-loser-leaves-town.

20   Benigno.

23   "Dwayne 'The Rock' Johnson on Raising Daughter Simone: I 'Lead Our Life with Love,'" *People*, December 3, 2020, https://people.com/parents/dwayne-johnson-the-rock-raising-daughter-simone-oprah-master-class/.

24   "WWE: The Rock's Daughter, Simone Johnson, Will Step into the Ring," BBC, February 12, 2020, https://www.bbc.com/news/newsbeat-51471305.

25   Roger Ebert, "The Scorpion King," RogerEbert.com, April 19, 2002, https://www.rogerebert.com/reviews/the-scorpion-king-2002.

28   Peter Hartlaub, "The Rock Is No More. Dwayne Johnson Has Fled the Ring, and Now He's Back on Familiar Turf: the Football Field," *SFGate*, September 14, 2006, https://www.sfgate.com /entertainment/article/The-Rock-is-no-more-Dwayne-Johnson -has-fled-the-2487861.php.

29   Cole Smithey, "Gridiron Gang," ColeSmithey.com, September 27, 2006, https://www.colesmithey.com/capsules/2006/09/gridiron _gang.html.

31   Nick de Semlyen, "*Fast & Furious 5: Rio Heist* Review," *Empire*, April 20, 2011, https://www.empireonline.com/movies/reviews /fast-furious-5-rio-heist-review/.

34–35 Eric Deggans, "USA's 'Mr. Robot,' HBO's 'Ballers' among Picks for Best Summer TV Series," NPR.com, July 1, 2015, https://www. npr.org/2015/07/01/418936119/usas-mr-robot-hbos-ballers -among-picks-for-best-summer-tv-series.

39   Dave Itzkoff, "Dwayne Johnson Finds Room to Grow in '*Young Rock*,'" *New York Times*, February 15, 2021, https://www .nytimes.com/2021/02/15/arts/television/dwayne-johnson-young -rock.html.

SELECTED BIBLIOGRAPHY

DK. *WWE Encyclopedia of Sports Entertainment.* London: DK, 2020.

Garcia, Hiram. *The Rock: Through His Lens: His Life, His Movies, His World.* New York: St. Martin's, 2020.

Johnson, Dwayne, and Joseph Layden. *The Rock Says . . . .* New York: HarperCollins, 2000.

Shipnuck, Alan. "How Football Helped Transform Dwayne Johnson into Hollywood's Biggest Star." SI.com, November 30, 2016. https://www.si.com/media/2016/11/30/dwayne-johnson-the-rock-nfl-wrestling-hollywood-star.

LEARN MORE

Black, Jake. *WWE Superstar Handbook: The Essential Facts and Stats on More Than 300 WWE Superstars!* New York: DK, 2021.

How Pro Wrestling Works
https://entertainment.howstuffworks.com/pro-wrestling.htm

Levit, Joseph. *Pro Wrestling's G.O.A.T.: Hulk Hogan, Dwayne "The Rock" Johnson, and More.* Minneapolis: Lerner Publications, 2022.

Santos, Rita. *Dwayne "The Rock" Johnson: Pro Wrestler and Actor.* New York: Enslow, 2020.

Sports Illustrated Kids: Wrestling
https://www.sikids.com/wrestling

World Wrestling Entertainment: The Rock
https://www.wwe.com/superstars/the-rock

INDEX